THE FIVE DYSFUNCTIONS OF A TEAM

(MANGA EDITION):

AN ILLUSTRATED LEADERSHIP FABLE

BY PATRICK LENCIONI

THE FIVE DYSFUNCTIONS OF A TEAM (MANGA EDITION): AN ILLUSTRATED LEADERSHIP FABLE

BY PATRICK LENCIONI

ILLUSTRATED BY KENSUKE OKABAYASHI

JOSSEY-BASS™
An Imprint of
WILEY

This edition published in 2008 by John Wiley & Sons (Asia) Pte Ltd., 2 Clementi Loop, #02-01, Singapore 129809.

Jossey-Bass books and products are available through most bookstores. To contact Jossey-Bass directly call our Customer Care Department within the U.S. at 800-956-7739, outside the U.S. at 317-572-3986, or fax 317-572-4002.

Jossey-Bass also publishes its books in a variety of electronic formats. Some content that appears in print may not be available in electronic books.

Library of Congress Cataloging-in-Publication Data

ISBN: 978-0470-82338-5

Edited by Douglas W. Jackson, Fresh Eyes Communications
Printed and bound in Great Britain by Bell & Bain Ltd, Glasgow
B823385R1_260225

Table of CONTENTS

THE FABLE

Part One: Underachievement 1

Part Two: Lighting the Fire 8

Part Three: Heavy Lifting 91

Part Four: Traction 140

THE MODEL

Dysfunction 1: Absence of Trust 153

Dysfunction 2: Fear of Conflict 157

Dysfunction 3: Lack of Commitment 162

Dysfunction 4: Avoidance of Accountability 166

Dysfunction 5: Inattention to Results 170

PART 1 - Underachievement

Situated near San Francisco in a little coastal town called Half Moon Bay, DecisionTech wasn't in Silicon Valley. The Valley's mostly a state of mind, though, and in that sense DecisionTech was pure Silicon.

The software company boasted a savvy, high-priced executive team, shatterproof business plan, and tons of top-tier investors. Alpha geeks from all over were begging to get on board.

Yep, DecisionTech had it all.

That was nearly two years ago, though, and the euphoria was long gone. The Valley grapevine had DecisionTech pegged as a nasty, depressing place to work. Morale was crumbling.

On the firm's two-year anniversary, they canned 37-year-old co-founder and CEO Jeff Shanley.

Another board of directors might have propped up their stumbling executive crew, but DecisionTech's couldn't stomach the bad press—not when the future had been so bright.

Jeff's dismissal didn't shock anybody.

His team had no unity or camaraderie, and backstabbing was the new executive sport of choice. Nothing ever seemed to get done, or at least done properly.

Jeff grabbed the board's offer to make him head of business development, eyes on the huge pay-out an IPO might bring. Even in the Valley's arid economic climate, DecisionTech still had IPO potential.

Everyone seemed relieved that Jeff was out—at least until Kathryn Petersen was named to replace him.

1

kathryn

Typically, DecisionTech's executive team couldn't even agree on which part of Kathryn's bio appealed least.

Oh, great, she was in the military. Everybody ready for your boot camp experience?

A B-school degree from Cal State Hayward's night program—wow, color me impressed.

There's no real high-tech experience on her resume. How's she going to get what we do here?

Just another old school, blue-collar exec. And she's a retiree!

Kathryn and DecisionTech looked like a total mismatch.

Even the board was questioning the chairman's sanity.

The man's instincts about people have always been sharp.

True, but he blew it when he made Jeff the CEO. Are we looking at two in a row here?

The chairman, however, flatly assured them that Kathryn would succeed.

Look, we're lucky that someone of Kathryn's caliber is even available.

Kathryn was floored when the chairman offered her the job.

I've known you for a long time, Stan, ever since my husband coached your son Dan in basketball, but what could you possibly know about my executive skills?

As it turned out, quite a lot.

I've been tracking your career for years. I saw how you turned that U.S.–Japanese JV auto manufacturing plant in the Bay Area into one of the most successful cooperative enterprises in the country.

I know zip about the car business, but I know talent, and you've got a particular gift for building teams. That's exactly what we need to turn DecisionTech around.

He finally persuaded Kathryn to take the position.

Her first two weeks on the job, however, had DecisionTech's execs baffled and uneasy.

Aside from attending a welcome reception and interviewing her direct reports, Kathryn just walked the halls, chatted with employees, and observed meetings.

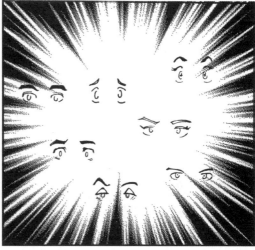

She even let Jeff Shanley lead the executive staff meetings while she sat back and took notes.

So what is this, leadership by lack of example?

Apparently.

Kathryn's only true executive decision—setting up a series of two-day offsite retreats in the Napa Valley—upset her team even more.

WELCOME to this world famous wine growing region

This is totally bogus! Does she realize how much work we've got facing us?

Kathryn's obviously got a faulty logic board.

PERFORMANCE FEEDBACK

The feedback the chairman was getting about Kathryn's performance surprised and unnerved him.

If Kathryn blows this, looks like I'll be heading for the exit, too.

the staff

After observing DecisionTech's dysfunctional executive family firsthand, Kathryn wondered if she'd made a titanic mistake.

Not that she regretted jumping back into the game. Kathryn loved a challenge, and she wasn't afraid of these Silicon Valley yuppies. She'd aced military life, dealt with hormone-charged kids, and even faced down union bosses.

She was also sure she knew enough about high tech and enterprise software to pull DecisionTech out of its death spiral.

COMPANY DECISION TECH

Still, the DecisionTech gig felt different. And the downside possibilities—failing the chairman, ending a solid career with a black mark—had her spooked in spite of herself.

And maybe not knowing too much was a plus. Her staff's techno-mastery actually seemed to intensify their paralysis.

Well, Jack Welch didn't have to know about toasters to make GE work.

Kathryn's executive team, however, would prove to be even more screwed up than anyone had imagined.

DecisionTech employees always called the executives "The Staff." The word *team* never entered the conversation.

That was no accident. These people were smart and had the degrees and deeds to prove it, but they acted worse than the seventh graders she'd taught—the room vibrated with tension, constructive exchanges were rare, and nothing got settled.

Yet as individuals, they seemed to be mostly reasonable, well-intentioned people.

Former CEO Jeff Shanley was a wizard at conjuring up venture capital and wooing talent. As a manager, however, he was definitely a poster boy for the Peter Principle.

Michele "Mikey" Bebe, DecisionTech's marketing VP, was a brand-building genius but socially clueless. She regularly dissed her colleagues and consequently ranked low on the internal popularity chart.

Martin Gilmore, a DecisionTech founder and the company's chief technologist, was a Brit whose brilliance was overshadowed by his tendency to make snide comments at meetings and contribute little else.

The head of sales was Jeff Rawlins, whom everyone called JR. Although JR was a sales veteran he was a bit flaky, rarely following up on his promises with action.

Carlos Amador headed up DecisionTech's customer support. Carlos was helpful, modest, listened intently and spoke rarely, but always had something pertinent and constructive to add when he did.

Jan Mersino, DecisionTech's chief financial officer, had helped Jeff raise the cash that launched the company. Thoughtful and thorough, Jan treated the company's money like it was her own.

COO Nick Farrell was a former field operations VP at a big Midwest computer maker. DecisionTech's sputtering start had pre-empted Nick's primary duties, bruising his ego and frustrating him immensely.

Martin's email looked innocent enough, but Kathryn immediately spotted its incendiary potential.

Addressed to the whole executive team, the message said:

MAIL

ASA Manufacturing is thinking about a purchase next quarter and wants to review our product. JR and I are going out there next weevk.
Be back Tuesday.
Cheers,
Martin

SA Manufacturing is th
a purchase next quarter a
to review our product. JR
going out there next week.
Be back Tuesday.
Chee
M

Kathryn sighed. No mention of the date conflict with the Napa off-site. No request to miss the retreat's first day and a half, and no apology.

This is either a low-key mutiny or conflict avoidance. Either way, Martin, you're not blowing this off so easily.

DECISION

MARTIN GILM

9

At lunch . . .

Knowing what was coming, Kathryn preempted Jeff.

Thanks so much for leading the meetings, Jeff. I really appreciated the chance to sit back and observe.

After next week's off-site, though, I'll take over. Please keep contributing, though—I value your input.

Uh, thanks, Kathryn.

Since you bring up the off-site, I've got a question.

Sure, what is it?

Well, I was talking to Martin in the parking lot yesterday . . .

. . . and, um, he mentioned the ASA meeting and the scheduling conflict.

And?

Well, Martin believes—and I agree—that the ASA meeting outranks the off-site. I mean, missing the first day or so shouldn't be that big a deal.

Jeff, I'm not here to run you down, and I know you really care about this company . . .

11

drawing the line

Kathryn had foreseen some internal fallout from her encounter with Martin, so the lunch with Jeff hadn't fazed her. The source of the next pointed inquiry, however, was a shock—the chairman.

PETERSON

BZZZZZZZZ

Kathryn, I just spoke with Jeff.

So you know about me butting heads with Martin, then.

Yes, and I'm concerned.

Really?

Frankly, yes. I don't want to tell you how to operate, but . . .

. . . I think you'd be better off building some bridges before you burn any.

Stan, may I be blunt with you?

All right.

Kathryn quickly shifted into CEO mode.

I've been watching this crew carefully for the past two weeks. I'm not setting fires at random here.

I'm sure that's true. It's just that—

Wait, please hear me out.

Okay, shoot.

If you knew how to do this team voodoo thing, you wouldn't need me, right?

Right.

For the past eighteen months you've been very hands-on with Jeff and the team. You know they're totally dysfunctional.

The chairman sat back, letting scenarios run through his mind.

And now you've asked me to pull them out of that spiral, right?

Then I've got one question: Are you ready for the collateral damage that's coming?

Nobody's life is at stake, but careers and reputations are. This isn't going to be pretty, Stan, not for the company, the team, for me . . .

. . . or for you.

You know my husband says a broken team is like a broken arm—sometimes you've got to re-break it before it heals right.

OK, I get your drift, Kathryn. Do what you've got to do. But I've got a question of my own . . .

. . . How much of this team are you going to have to break?

I should know that by the end of the month.

Kathryn chose the Napa Valley for the off-sites because it was close to the office but far enough away to feel like they were going out of town.

WELCOME to this worldfamous wine growing region

NAPA VALLEY

...and the wine is bottled poetry...

More importantly, people always slowed down a pace or two there.

The hotel, The Vinland Vale Inn, was a cozy place in the little burg of Yountville.

The inn had just one big, comfortable conference room, with a balcony that overlooked acres of vineyards.

the speech

We're going to begin addressing this issue over the next few days.

I know it seems crazy to be out of the office for so long, but when we're finished everybody that's still here will know why it's absolutely essential.

That got everyone's undivided attention.

That's right. DecisionTech will be going through some changes, and a few of us probably won't like the new direction.

Again, I don't have anybody in mind, and I'm not making threats or being dramatic.

Just consider this a reality check.

Everybody here is eminently employable,

And the world won't end if saying goodbye is the right thing for the company—and this team.

The sole goal of these retreats is to produce results. To me, that's the only true measure of a team.

We're not here to hold hands, sing songs . . .

. . . or get naked together. Trust me on that.

23

Wait, so no debate equals lack of trust? That doesn't compute.

No, not necessarily, I guess.

Nick grinned, but his victory was short-lived.

In a perfect world, Nick, we'd all be on the same page, and zero conflict would be the norm. But this isn't *Star Trek*, and we're not Borg drones.

Every effective team I've seen mixes it up verbally. So why don't we? Our goals are out of sync and we're clearly in trouble, so why isn't anybody saying so?

Mikey muttered under her breath.

Sorry, Mikey, I didn't catch that.

I said, "Nobody has the time."

In case you hadn't noticed, Kathryn, we're all way too busy and stressed to hassle each other over minor issues.

I don't know about that, Mikey. Maybe we're just not comfortable confronting each other. I'm not sure why, though.

Oh, gee, could it be because our meetings are so structured and boring?

Wait a sec. Yeah, our meetings are usually less than thrilling and the agendas are overstuffed, but we could challenge each other more.

We sure don't agree on everything.

Actually, Carlos, I don't think we agree on anything!

HA HA HA HA HA HA HA

I'm certainly no psychologist, but that sounds like a trust issue to me.

You guys don't agree, but you won't even admit that you've got troubles.

tap tap tap tap tap tap tap tap tap tap tap tap tap tap

Martin had started banging away on his keyboard, and it was killing the conversational momentum.

27

getting naked

The session's first item was deceptively straightforward.

Before we begin the heavy lifting, let's try an exercise I call "personal histories."

I'll ask you a few simple questions that always seem to produce amazing responses.

Oh, and we want to hear about your life as a child, *not* your inner child.

5 Questions

1. Hometown?
2. Number of kids in the family?
3. Interesting childhood hobbies?
4. Biggest challenge growing up?
5. First job?

One by one, the seven execs revealed details about their hometowns, families, hobbies, challenges and first jobs. Kathryn's prediction was spot on.

Carlos was the oldest of nine kids.

Mikey had studied ballet at the Juilliard School in New York.

Jeff was a bat boy for the Boston Red Sox.

When the team came back, they'd obviously lost some of the morning session's glow.

Despite that, everyone spent several hours sharing their responses to behavioral tools like the Myers-Briggs Type Indicator, which they'd all completed before coming to Napa.

As they worked through lunch, Kathryn was pleased to see that even Martin was into it. Then again, she thought, people love to talk about themselves.

It'd be different when the criticism began.

With energy levels dropping and the rest of the night to go, Kathryn gave the team what was left of the afternoon off.

Martin pored over his e-mail.

DO NOT DIST URB

Nick, Jeff, Carlos and JR played some bocce ball.

Kathryn met with Jan to talk about budgets.

Mikey lounged by the pool and read some pulp fiction.

31

When they got back, Kathryn was happy to see the conversation resuming right where they'd left off. By now, everyone had figured out their individual working styles as well as the implications of being an extrovert or introvert and other personality quirks.

All the beer and pizza had relaxed the group, and they were ribbing each other good-naturedly.

BEER BEER

CHIPS CHIPS

Even Martin responded with a grin when Nick called him a "raging introvert."

Nobody was teasing her, and Mikey sure wasn't tossing around any jibes of her own.

Jeff razzed JR for being unfocused.

No one at the table was fazed by the good-natured ribbing . . . except Mikey.

Kathryn's first impulse was to drag Mikey into the verbal scrum, but she wanted to avoid fireworks on the first day.

As it turned out, Mikey set off the fireworks all by herself, rolling her eyes when Nick commented about how accurate and helpful the personality descriptions were.

33

For a moment Kathryn thought her marketing VP might storm out.

What she did was worse—slouching down, sulky and unresponsive, as the conversation veered into the realm of business tactics.

Jan broke in with a question.

We're not getting off-topic, are we?

No, I'm all for diving into operational issues while we're exploring the behavioral stuff.

In fact, it should help us figure out how translate our ideas into action items.

Kathryn loved the interaction she was seeing, but the Mikey spoiler effect was becoming a powerful drag.

If their marketing genius didn't start trusting her teammates, it was going to cost everyone.

poolside

The session ended around 10 p.m. Most of the team headed for bed. Since Kathryn and Mikey's rooms were both near the pool, Kathryn figured she'd try some damage control as they walked.

Just wonderful, thanks.

Are you okay?

Look, Mikey, this process has edges. I know they were a little tough on you in there.

A little?!

I don't take that kind of crap from anybody, even at home! These guys don't have a clue about what makes a company successful.

What is this woman thinking?

Well, why not tell them how you feel? That's what this off-site is all about.

Oh, I'm not saying a single word tomorrow.

39

And it probably pisses you guys off.

Sounds like your strength and weakness are the same, Nick.

Isn't that usually the case?

That's exactly the kind of input I'm after. Next?

Jan volunteered, citing her management skills and attention to detail as pluses but admitting she was more financially conservative than a startup's CFO should be.

I guess my experience at big firms did that. But I need to stop riding you guys so hard.

Carlos reassured her.

Believe me, Jan, we can meet you halfway.

Jeff went next, but struggled to come up with what everyone already recognized—his amazing skills at networking and building partnerships with investors and others.

41

Mikey sat back down just as abruptly.

Relief that Mikey was finished mixed with disappointment at her shallow responses and offhand manner.

Kathryn thought about pushing her for more, but decided against it.

Carlos broke the tense silence.

Okay, me next.

Follow-through is my big strength.

Carlos, I think you're wrong on both scores. Your real strength is your willingness to do the dirty work and not complain.

What I'm really bad at is updating people on what I'm doing and whether I'm making progress.

I know that sounds terrible, but things would be even worse without you bailing us out all the time.

On the negative side, you hold back too much at meetings. You always provide good input.

JR followed.

Well, my biggest strength is clearly follow-through and attention to detail!

The room rocked with laughter.

Seriously, though, I'm great at building close relationships with customers.

My bad habit is that I sometimes blow off stuff that doesn't help me close a deal.

44

49

That's harsh.

Maybe. But the next season Donny showed up with a brand-new attitude. He went on to play for St. Mary's College. He'll tell you that that year was the most important of his life.

So you think people like that can really change?

Well, maybe one kid out of ten.

Ken always tells me his job is to put together the best team possible, not mold superstars. That's how I look at my job, too.

Did anybody here play team sports in high school or college?

Nick said he'd played baseball in college.

Carlos was a linebacker in high school.

I played football, too—the original kind.

Mikey said she ran track in high school.

51

Maybe not so many, but the ones that are have a huge advantage over the guys who are just out for themselves.

What's this got to do with a software company, anyway?

Everything, Mikey.

Don't we already have a scoreboard?

We're going to make DecisionTech's collective results as important as the final score in a game. Group success beats individual ego.

You mean profit?

Yeah. What else is there?

Now I'm confused!

Sure, profit's big, but profit alone won't tell you how the team is doing until the season's over. I'm thinking about near-term results.

Isn't profit the only score that matters?

53

goals

Kathryn formed groups of two and three and asked everyone to come up with categories for a team scoreboard.

CONFERENCE ROOM

They identified fifteen results categories, then pared the list down to seven:

revenue
expenses
new customer acquisition
customer satisfaction
employee retention
market
awareness
product quality.

To make detecting glitches and switching strategies easier, they decided to assess results monthly rather than quarterly.

These metrics are basically the same ones we've been using for nine months, Kathryn.

With the talk turning to business, the mood got serious.

Yeah, and revenue's still flat. Unless we close some deals, and fast, they're meaningless.

Kathryn stared at her lap, then looked back up.

Jan, you're absolutely right. Thanks for calling me on it.

Guess I just don't feel like I'm part of the group yet.

Hey, join the club.

Why would you say that?

Well, at my other jobs I was always tapped into sales and operations. Here I feel isolated, like finance is its own little island.

Carlos nodded.

Yeah, at staff meetings it's like everybody's either lobbying for more resources or dodging stuff outside their territory. We never seem to have any common goals, either.

And you guys think I'm such a prince for volunteering, but at places I used to work everybody did that.

Wow, the politics here astound me—like some covert agency where everything is vague and secretive. That makes achieving overall goals hard, and focusing on personal success way too easy.

OK, so we're not the healthiest group of executives in the Valley . . .

. . . but political? That's really an overstatement, Kathryn.

I disagree.

In fact, this is the most political group I've ever seen.

Jeff took issue with that.

Maybe that's because you're new to high tech.

Plenty of companies I've worked at are more political than DecisionTech.

Yeah, from what I've heard we're about average. Besides, this market is tough.

Mikey pounced.

That's a pretty careless remark, Kathryn, considering you've only been here a few weeks!

61

Silence . . .

Well then, we're definitely political.

Although Martin's comment hadn't been meant as a joke, it broke the tension.

Kathryn waited for more reaction. Were they going to embrace the idea, or fight her on this?

Her answer wasn't long in coming.

attack

No. He'd let them argue the point first, though, and tell them exactly why he disagreed.

So you're saying this isn't a consensus thing?

Far from it. True consensus is depressingly rare. There's a whole lotta faking going on. It's mostly an attempt to appease everybody—

Jeff, obviously reliving some bad moments, finishes Kathryn's thought.

—that usually ends up upsetting everybody.

Right. Fortunately, reasonable people usually just want their input considered.

Okay, so where does lack of commitment come into play?

The need for a unanimous verdict paralyzes a lot of teams. They can't commit.

CONFLICT

Oh, I get it. You're talking about disagree and commit.

What's that, JR?

Basically, you can disagree about a move but commit to it like everyone had bought into the decision completely.

Okay, I guess I see where conflict fits in. But even if people are willing to commit, they won't, because . . .

Carlos completes Jeff's thought.

. . . because they need to weigh in before they'll buy in, right?

Everyone seemed to grasp the point.

So what's the last dysfunction, Kathryn?

Everyone's shocked to realize that Mikey is the one asking the question. Could she actually be getting into the spirit here?

Ah, like telling someone to shut down their laptop during a meeting, I suppose?

Exactly!

I hate that. Rather than tell someone their standards are too low, I'd just tolerate it and . . .

. . . avoid the interpersonal discomfort?

Yeah, I suppose so.

What's weird is that I never hesitate to jump on my direct reports when they screw up.

Right.

Getting into it with your peers is a lot tougher, isn't it?

Why's that?

Nick jumps in before Kathryn can explain.

Because we're supposed to be equals. And everybody's got their own MO. Besides, who am I to tell Mikey or Martin or whoever how to do their jobs?

film noir

Why can't we ever just settle things in one fell swoop?

In theory, having Martin and Mikey on board should make turning this team around simple.

Kathryn had formed and reformed plenty of teams, but the inevitable ebbs and flows they went through still baffled her.

Kathryn was tempted to cut the off-site short and send everyone home feeling good, but she couldn't toss away those two hours.

In real life, one session couldn't wipe away two years of political infighting. The heavy lifting was yet to come.

The more progress she made, the less likely it was that the board would cut her reforms short.

After the group reassembled, she went back to a topic guaranteed to keep everyone's attention.

Let's talk some more about conflict.

77

I never got an agenda.

HA HA HA HA HA HA HA HA HA HA

Everyone—including Jeff himself—laughed at the good-natured teasing of DecisionTech's former CEO.

CONFLICT!!

application

81

Okay, new customer acquisition.

NEW CUSTOMERS

Why should this be our big collective goal?

It'll give the media something to write about, and boost morale. Martin and his crew will get more product feedback. And we'll have references that make it easier to get more customers next year.

Don't forget follow-on sales.

Folks, unless I hear something even more compelling in the next five seconds, I believe we have our primary goal.

Okay, so how many new customers do we need?

Invigorated by the positive nature of the discussion, the group debated the question for the next thirty minutes.

Jan lobbied for the most, with Nick and Mikey not far behind.

JR argued for the fewest, wanting to keep the pressure off his sales people.

Carlos and Martin were somewhere in between.

It looks like the votes are in. We're not all going to love the final number, but that's okay. Disagree and commit, right?

Jan, I know you'd love the revenue, but we won't do thirty deals this year.

And JR, ten just isn't enough. Our competitors are more than doubling that, and the analysts will eat our lunch if that's all we can manage.

If we can close eighteen new customers, with at least ten willing to act as references, I think we'll be doing well.

Nobody disagreed.

Goal by December 31

So it's settled. By December 31, we will have eighteen new customers.

The group seemed relieved to be finished.

unghh. . .

Kathryn asked one final question.

yawwn

Are there any final comments, questions or concerns to bring up before we leave?

Please, no more! My brain is fried!

Just a comment— we made more progress these past two days than I imagined we would.

Maybe Nick was just trying to score points, but Kathryn decided to take the compliment at face value.

PART 3 - Heavy Lifting

Even Kathryn was stunned by how quickly the progress they had made at the off-site vanished.

The few glimmers of hope—like Carlos and Martin doing a customer satisfaction evaluation with their combined staffs—had DecisionTech's employees frantically trading rumors and speculation, but her executives were in lockdown mode.

Based on their hallway demeanor, it was like the off-site had never happened. There was no interaction and no engagement.

They seemed self-conscious about how much of themselves they'd exposed at Napa.

That the group hadn't internalized the concepts was frustrating, but Kathryn knew this was a typical first response.

The only way to bring them back online was to get their blood pumping again. She had no idea her strategy would hit an artery.

It happened the day of Kathryn's first official staff meeting. Nick had called for a special meeting to discuss a possible acquisition, specifically asking Kathryn, Martin, JR and Jeff to attend.

Jan and Carlos showed up as well.

Where's JR?

He's out this morning. Let's get started.

Okay, the company is in Boston, and it's called Green Banana.

Everyone laughed.

Yeah, I know—you've gotta wonder how they come up with these names.

Anyway, they're either a good match for us or a potential rival.

Tough to say which, but I'd like us to consider buying them. They're hurting for cash, and we've got more than we need.

What would we get?

Customers, employees, technology.

How many customers?

And their technology's good? I've never heard of them.

About twenty, I think, and those customers seem to like their tech well enough.

Martin looked skeptical. Kathryn frowned.

How many people do they have? Are they all in Boston?

Around seventy-five, and all but seven are based in Beantown.

This deal sounds risky to me, Nick. We'd be adding 50 percent more staff and a whole new line of products. Don't we have enough challenges already?

Nick couldn't mask his frustration.

We've got to be visionaries!

We've got to make some bold moves to pull away from the competition, Kathryn!

Mikey should really be here. I'd like to know what she says about the effect on market positioning and strategy, and—

95

Well, I could be macho and say "Let's do it right here," but in private is probably better.

Please excuse us, everyone. We'll see you at the staff meeting.

First of all, Nick, never slam a colleague when they're not around.

I don't care what you think of Mikey. She's part of this team, and you either deal with her directly or speak to me.

Look, I've got nothing to do around here. We should be bursting at the seams by now—new branches, M&A, all that.

So this is about you?

What?

This acquisition. Is it to give you something to do?

No, it's a good strategic move for us.

But what Nick said next revealed his true fears.

I moved my family halfway across the country figuring I'd be running this place soon. Now I'm bored, under utilized and watching my peers screw everything up!

And you've got nothing to do with that?

No! I mean, I'm handling M&A and infrastructure growth—or at least I'm supposed to be.

96

The board says we can't right now, so—

I'm talking about the bigger picture, Nick.

Are you making this team better, or just adding to the dysfunction?

What do you think?

You clearly have a lot to offer, and you may end up running this place.

But right now you're not making it better.

I wasn't saying I want your job. I was just venting and—

It's okay to vent from time to time, Nick.

But I don't see you stepping up and helping. If anything, you're tearing people down.

So what should I be doing?

Tell us where you're coming from—that you feel underused and frustrated.

That has nothing to do with buying Green Banana.

They both chuckled briefly at the ridiculous name. Then Nick got serious again.

If they don't understand why we need to do that, maybe—

Maybe what? Maybe you should quit?

The staff meeting started at 2 p.m., minus Nick and JR.

Okay, let's quickly review what everyone is working on and then start laying the groundwork for those eighteen deals we need to close.

Sorry I'm late!

Nick chose the seat furthest away from Kathryn.

Before we get started, I need to—

Hold on a sec!

I need to get some things off my chest.

First, I was out of line this morning.

The comment I made about Mikey wasn't fair . . .

. . . and I shouldn't have said anything unless it was face to face.

It's not that big a deal, Mikey. I'll tell you about it later.

Second, although I still think we should consider buying Green Banana, I guess the deal is more about me having something to work on.

. . . .

See, I'm wondering if I made a bad career move by coming here.

The last eighteen months are basically a blank on my resume. Having nothing to do is driving me nuts.

I have to find a way to contribute to this team and this company, and I need your help on that.

If I can't, I should leave.

But I'm not ready to do that yet.

Nobody knew what to say, although Kathryn silently congratulated Nick for being so open.

Besides, she had a bombshell of her own.

I need to make an announcement.

JR quit last night.

What?! Why?

I'm still not sure, even after speaking to him directly.

He's going back to his old position as regional VP at AddSoft.

He did say he didn't want to waste his time at retreats working out people's problems.

Carlos, we know you always step up, but two people here have more sales experience and more time for it—

Jeff and Nick.

Well, I've never run a sales group or carried a quota, but I'll do it if I'm with someone who knows what they're doing.

But when we interviewed him, Nick said he didn't want to be a field guy anymore.

Nick, you ran field operations at your last job, and headed a sales team before that.

Yeah, I felt I was being pigeonholed.

But I was damned good at sales, and I enjoyed it.

Jeff spoke up.

You've already got a good relationship with the sales force, and I know you're frustrated with our lack of deals.

Come on, Nick.

If you don't do it, they'll have to accept my offer!

leaks

A few days later, Kathryn's laptop started acting up. She called the IT department to get it fixed.

IT had just four staff. Brendan, the head, was one of Jan's direct reports.

Brendan often handled calls himself, especially if the call came from the CEO.

He checked the laptop and told Kathryn he'd have to take it with him.

Fine, but I'll need it back before the weekend.

Oh, right— you've got another off-site.

His next remarks dismayed Kathryn.

Man, I'd love to be a fly on the wall at that session.

Really? Why?

Anyway, thanks for taking care of my machine, Brendan.

Let's just say that people would pay to watch Mikey answer for her attitude.

Ahh, that's not how I'd describe what we've been doing.

As Brendan left, Kathryn wondered how many other people were hearing stories about Napa.

Yes, that's what prompted me to ask the question.

But this isn't about anyone in particular. I'm trying to get a handle on our loyalties.

Our loyalties? Meaning what, exactly?

Meaning who do you consider to be your first team?

Confidentiality isn't the focus here.

What I want to talk about goes way beyond that.

Basically, I want to know if this team is as important to you as the one you lead.

You're wondering if we tell our direct reports stuff that should stay between us here?

That's part of it, yes.

I'm much closer to my staff than this group. Sorry, but it's true.

Me too, except for the sales group I just took over. And in a few weeks I'll be closer to them as well.

Nick meant it as a joke, but it was true.

We all feel the same, I bet. But no one more than me.

Why do you say that, Jan?

Well, everyone knows I'm tight with my people. Five of my eight direct reports worked for me at other companies.

Yeah, Jan's a den mother.

It's true. I don't fuss over them, but they know I'd do almost anything for them.

I'm the same. I protect my engineers from interference and distractions, and in return they work their tails off for me.

Kathryn nodded as if she'd just figured something out.

Mine don't quit, even when things get tough.

Of course not. I'm glad you feel so strongly about your people. That jibes with what I learned during our initial interviews.

Now you're going to tell us that being a good manager is a flaw or something, right?

OK, so what's the problem?

Unfortunately, good managers who don't act like a team create a dilemma for themselves and the company.

First team?

Specifically, confusion about who their first team is.

Right. Remember the last dysfunction—putting team results ahead of individual issues? There's no question that loyalty to your staff is wonderful . . .

. . . but it can't supersede your loyalty and commitment to the people sitting at this table. We have to be your first team.

This is a tough one, Kathryn.

I don't think you have to abandon them, Jan.

No, you don't have to destroy that bond . . .

I could give you a half-assed assurance that this is now my first team, but I'd feel like I was abandoning my own people.

. . . but you have to be willing to make your team secondary to this one.

For many of you, that may feel like abandonment.

Jeff tried to lighten the mood.

Now you can see why building a team is so hard.

Hey, think how crappy I feel. You guys always were my first team, so I never had anyone else to listen to my bitching!

Kathryn saw skepticism on their faces, but their doubts were clearly about whether they could pull it off, not whether making this team paramount was important. And she was okay with that.

plowing on

Well, we won't solve this one today, so let's just stick to our goal of building a solid team.

Maybe then the prospect of making this team your top priority won't seem so daunting.

So how are we doing?

Well, if you'd told me JR would quit and that we'd already have Nick in his place, I'd think you engineered the whole scenario.

And I never thought I'd be doing this job, or having so much fun.

But how are we working as a team?

We're headed in the right direction, I think. There's definitely more productive conflict.

HA
HA
HA
HA
HA

I'm—I'm having my doubts.

Well, I feel like we're still not talking about the big issues.

Why is that, Carlos?

Such as?

I don't want to stir things up here . . .

Please, stir away.

OK. I'm wondering if our resources are distributed right.

Martin sensed that Carlos had his department in mind. And he was right.

Engineering's got so many people, like a third of the company.

Sales, marketing and consulting could use some help.

Martin liked to use the Socratic method—with a sarcastic twist—to attack comments he didn't like. Before he could open his mouth, though, Mikey spoke.

I agree with Carlos. Frankly, I don't know what half our engineers are up to!

Here we go again!

sighh . . .

And money to upgrade our marketing and ad campaigns—mmm, makes me salivate just thinking about it.

Okay, let's wrestle with this one.

This is not civil war, though. It's about strategy.

First, we owe it to our employees and shareholders to use our money wisely.

You're damned right I am!!

Martin, I'm guessing you're sick of people questioning our investment in engineering.

Nobody gets that we're investing in technology and developing products! I'm not taking my engineers out to play golf, for God's sake.

C'mon, Martin, everybody knows engineers don't play golf!

Anyway, we aren't saying you're fiscally irresponsible, just a bit . . . biased.

Biased? I do as many sales calls as anyone here, speak to analysts—

Jan jumped in.

Nobody's questioning your commitment to DecisionTech.

But you know more about engineering than anything else, so it's natural that you want to plow money back into the product.

Anyway, why do you get so defensive when we comment about engineering?

Yeah. You act like we're questioning your intelligence.

Aren't you? Like I don't know how much it costs to build and maintain our product?

No, we're questioning how good our products need to be to win in the market, and how much we'll have to invest in future technology.

You can't figure out that alone, Martin. Nobody can. We need the whole team's perspective.

Listen, I don't want to read a bloody epitaph that pins our corporate demise on shoddy technology. We've put too much into it.

Martin immediately realized that his declaration was a textbook example of the fifth dysfunction.

Ahh . . . I admit that sounds like I'm more concerned about avoiding blame than helping the company win, but—

Martin halted, at a loss for words. Jan bailed him out.

Why do you think I'm so anal about our finances?

Because I never want to read in *The Wall Street Journal* that the company tanked because we didn't manage our cash properly.

The same with Carlos and customer support, Mikey with branding, and everybody else.

Mikey's expression said she clearly wasn't worried about that.

So are we all scrambling for the lifeboats on the *Titanic*?

Oh, we're not that desperate.

Well, it does seem we're all standing as close as possible just in case.

So where are we now, Martin?

Martin took a deep breath, shook his head as if disagreeing with all that had been said . . .

. . . and then surprised everyone by walking to the whiteboard.

Okay, let's hash this out.

He mapped out his entire organization, describing what everyone was working on and how the pieces interlocked.

The rest of the team was blown away, both by how much they didn't know about DecisionTech's engineering and how much was going on.

Kathryn gave the group two hours to determine whether engineering deserved more resources or fewer, and how to use any resources they freed up.

The team argued vehemently at times . . .

. . . changed their minds . . .

. . . and concluded the right answer wasn't so obvious or clear-cut.

Most important of all, everyone on the team—Kathryn included—went to the whiteboard to jot down a point or an idea.

If anyone yawned, it was because they were exhausted, not bored.

Finally, Jeff proposed a solution.

Let's cut one future product entirely, and delay another for at least six months.

Within minutes, the group had set an aggressive timeline for the change. They stared in amazement at the complex but workable solution on the whiteboard.

Nick suggested having the engineers from those projects trained to assist sales reps with product demonstrations.

Let's go to lunch. When we get back, we'll talk about dealing with interpersonal discomfort and holding each other accountable.

I can't wait.

119

Silence.

I'm not complaining. It's just that—

It's okay, Carlos, just tell me who needs to be more responsive.

Well, Jack's essential. And Ken. And I'm not sure if—

Kathryn interrupted.

Sorry, does anyone else see a problem here?

Yeah. I need to be clearer with my staff about our priorities and get them on board.

That's true, Nick. But what about Carlos?

Shouldn't he have mentioned this snag before today?

None of you tagged him when he confessed he hadn't even started the analysis.

It's hard to come down on someone who's always pitching in, I guess.

True. But Carlos is a VP, and he's responsible for keeping his priorities in line with our goals. If people aren't responding to his requests, he's got to say something—loud and clear.

121

Okay, item three—the sales training program. That's mine.

We're on pace, and I've scheduled a two-day training session. I think everyone should be there.

Why?!

Because if closing those deals is our top goal, we all have to be salespeople.

It is, Nick.

Good. So we all need to be involved, and know how to help our sales reps.

Mikey was obviously peeved.

Is there a problem, Mikey?

No, no. Go ahead.

If you've got a good reason not to be there, tell us.

Frankly, I can't imagine anything more critical.

Fine. I'd also like you all to attend next week's product marketing meeting.

Really? If you think it's essential, we'll be there.

Forget it. I'll be at the sales training, but I don't need any of you—other than Martin—at the product marketing meeting.

At that moment, Kathryn knew Mikey would have to go. Unfortunately, the next five minutes would make that much harder.

Nick moved to the fourth item on the list.

Okay, how's it going with the product brochures?

We're all set.

Really?

Yeah. This goes to the printer next week.

The room was quiet as everyone looked over the design and copy.

Kathryn could sense that most of them were impressed.

Nick, however, looked upset.

Were you going to talk to me first? My sales people are doing customer research for this.

They'll be miffed if their input is ignored . . .

125

Mikey seemed to have no clue what was coming. Would her ignorance make things easier or harder?

This is going to be a tough conversation, Mikey.

It is?

A flash of realization crossed Mikey's face.

Yes, and here's why. I don't think you fit in with this team. You don't even seem to want to be here.

Me?! You've got to be joking. Of all the people on this team, you think that I—

What's the basis for this?

You disrespect your colleagues and won't open up to them.

Your behavior is arrogant, dismissive and distasteful to everyone. Including me.

I don't respect my colleagues? More like they don't respect me!

Realizing she'd basically proved Kathryn's point, Mikey tried to clarify.

They don't appreciate my talent or my experience.

126

Kathryn's calm incensed Mikey.

Kathryn, what'll the board say if I leave? You already lost JR. I'd be worried about my job if I were you.

Thanks for your concern. Butting heads with the board is always a possibility. But I was hired to rebuild this executive team.

And I don't think you like being part of it.

So you figure getting rid of me will help?

Yes. And be better for you, too. Another firm might appreciate your skills and style more.

But I'd suggest taking a long look at yourself first.

What's that mean? I've never had problems like this before.

Well, if it's a DecisionTech thing, you'll no doubt be happier somewhere else.

Cornered, Mikey stared at the table. She finally appeared to grasp her situation, and even accept it.

Wrong.

127

last stand

Mikey excused herself to collect her thoughts. She came back more emotionally charged and determined than ever.

Okay, first off, I'm not quitting. You'll have to fire me. And my husband is a lawyer, so getting me out of here won't be easy.

But I'm not firing you, Mikey. You don't even have to leave.

However, your behavior would have to change radically—and in a hurry.

Frankly, I'm not sure you're up for that.

Mikey's expression made it clear that she wasn't.

Hey, *my* behavior isn't the problem.

It's just one of them, actually. You also never get involved in areas outside your department.

You can't deal with criticism from your peers, and you won't apologize when you're out of line.

Out of line? When?

Well, where to start . . .

129

All right, I want three months' severance and all my stock options vested.

I also want the record to show I resigned voluntarily.

I'll see if I can make that happen.

Mikey broke the awkward silence.

Should I just skip dinner and leave now?

That would probably be best. You can pick up your things next week and work with HR on your exit package.

You know you guys are screwed, don't you?

You have no sales or marketing people left. And I bet some of my staff will walk, too.

That could happen . . .

. . . but I hope it doesn't.

Kathryn spent the break taking a long walk around the vineyards.

Thus refreshed, she still wasn't prepared for what happened when the meeting resumed.

Where's Mikey?

Gone. She's leaving the company.

Clearly shocked, the team waited for more info.

All right, what I have to say is confidential, because of legal issues on departing staff.

Mikey's behavior was hurting the team. She wasn't prepared to change, so I asked her to leave.

The team members looked at each other, then at the brochures.

Wow. How did she take it? And what are we going to do about marketing?

What'll we tell the employees? And the media?

She was surprised, Carlos, and a little angry. About what you'd expect.

As far as our marketing goes, the search for a new VP starts now. We've got good people who can step up and keep us going until we find one. We'll tell the staff and the media that she's moving on. There'll be talk, but there always is.

If we get our act together and make progress, the employees and professional watchers will forget pretty fast.

Frankly, I don't think most people, especially the employees, will be surprised.

Kathryn's confidence and logic were both strong, but the team's mood stayed low. The Mikey issue clearly wasn't dead yet.

DecisionTech

Deepend II Enterprise Software BY MIKEY

heavy lifting

From that evening until the following afternoon, the group focused on business details, particularly sales.

They made progress, but Mikey's abrupt exit was still dampening the mood.

Kathryn decided to tackle the issue head-on.

We need to deal with the elephant in the room here—Mikey's departure.

I want to know how you're feeling about before I explain to the company next week.

Losing another member of the team worries me, I guess.

But Mikey never really was part of the team, was she?

Mikey was difficult, but she did great work. And marketing's so critical now—maybe we should have just put up with her.

Anyone else?

I'm just wondering . . . who's next?

Hmm. Okay, let me tell you a story—one I'm not proud of.

During my last quarter of grad school, I got a contract job running a small department of financial analysts at a well-known San Francisco retail company.

It was my first management position, and I was shooting for a job there after I graduated.

The people were all solid, but one—let's call him Fred—cranked out more reports, and better ones, than anybody. But he never helped the other analysts, and made sure they knew how much better he was at the job.

He became my most reliable employee.

I'd love to have that problem.

Wait for the rest of the story, Nick.

Several other analysts bitched about him. I listened, and even made some half-hearted attempts to change Fred's behavior.

Anyway, nobody could stand Fred, including me.

Mostly, though, I ignored them. They obviously resented his skills, and I wasn't about to come down on my top performer.

Eventually the department's output began dropping. I gave more work to Fred.

Performance and morale got worse. More people complained about Fred. I realized he was causing a lot of our problems.

After a lot of agonizing and a long, sleepless night, I made my first big management move.

You fired him!

Nope. I promoted him.

GASP!!

That's right. Fred was my first promotion as a manager. Two weeks later, three of my seven analysts quit. Chaos ensued. We dropped way behind schedule.

My manager called me in for a talk. I told him about Fred and the other analysts. The next day he made a decision of his own.

He fired Fred!

Close. He fired me.

But companies don't usually fire contractors.

Okay, let's just say my contract ended rather abruptly.

Nick and Martin were trying not to crack up.

ha ha ha ha ha
ha ha
ha ha ha
ha ha

I definitely got canned.

135

rally

Back at the office, Kathryn held an all-hands meeting to discuss Mikey's departure and other company issues.

The news provoked a surprising level of concern among DecisionTech's employees. The backlash was mostly reflex, but it did undercut the executive team's enthusiasm.

At the next staff meeting, they debated who would replace Mikey.

The prospect of promoting Ray, one of her direct reports, caused a heated dispute.

Kathryn stepped in to break the deadlock.

I don't think Ray or anyone else here matches that description, so we're going for an outside hire.

Jeff, please oversee the search.

As much as I'd prefer to promote internally, we need someone senior to grow the department and our brand.

Everybody here will be interviewing the candidates. I want you pressing them on all the dysfunction issues—trust, conflict, commitment, accountability and team results.

Seeing a budget request coming, Jan tried to head it off.

Nick then reported on sales.

We've made inroads with a few key prospects, but we're struggling in some regions. We need more feet on the street.

I'm against allocating money for this, Nick.

137

It just feels like we're fighting.

You are, but about issues. That's your job—hashing this stuff out so your people don't have to, and setting our direction.

I hope it's worth it.

Trust me, it will be—in more ways than you know.

For the next two weeks Kathryn pushed her team harder than ever.

She chided Martin for acting smug at meetings.

She battled with Jan and Nick over budgets, and forced Carlos to confront the team about their casual attitude on customer issues.

The team's reaction spoke volumes. No one questioned whether they should be doing what Kathryn asked. There was a real sense of collective purpose.

So how are we doing?

Inattention to Results — Status and Ego

Avoidance of Accountability — Low Standards

Lack of Commitment — Ambiguity

Fear of Conflict — Artificial Harmony

Absence Trust — nvulnerability

Well, we trust each other a lot more than we did a month ago.

But I'd say there's more work to be done.

We've got a lot more conflict going on, too. I'm still getting used to that.

Being comfortable with conflict is unlikely, but the discomfort proves it's real. We've just got to keep doing it.

Nick jumped in.

Why?

I'd say we're definitely getting better buy-in on objectives and deliverables. Accountability is what worries me.

Because I'm skeptical that we'll really get in each other's faces when someone doesn't deliver, or starts acting contrary to the good of the team.

Hey, *I'm* certainly going to get in their faces!

141

Martin's comment surprised everyone.

I'd hate to go back to the way things were. If it's interpersonal discomfort versus politics, I'm opting for discomfort.

Well, I don't think we'll have a results problem.

If we don't make this company work, none of us will smell rosy.

Kathryn had never been so happy to see a group of people all nodding in agreement.

But she decided it was time for a reality check.

I agree with most of what you're saying. Still, there will be days when you'll wonder if we've made any headway at all. And it'll be a while before this kicks in on the bottom line.

The team was agreeing a bit too readily.

143

By the end of the session, despite being clearly exhausted, they were all busy scheduling follow-up meetings to be held after they returned to the office.

GO TEAM, GO!!

gut check

Three months after the final offsite ended, Kathryn held her first quarterly staff meeting. The new marketing VP, Joseph Charles, had just joined DecisionTech. This was his first session with the group.

She kicked off the meeting with an unexpected announcement.

Hey, remember Green Banana, that company we considered buying?

Well, Nick was right—the company's a potential rival.

In fact, they want to buy us!

Huh? I thought they were in financial trouble!!

Apparently they raised a truckload of cash last month, and now they're hungry to spend it. They've already made us an offer.

What's it like?

Kathryn consulted her notes.

A lot more than our estimated worth. We'd all make decent money.

145

What did the board say?

That it's up to us.

No one spoke, but they were obviously all calculating payouts and futures. Then—

No bloody way!!

All heads turned to Martin.

HA HA HA HA HA HA HA HA HA HA HA

I'm not handing over all this to a company named after an unripened fruit!

Then Jan broke in.

Let's not discard this out of hand. This is real money, and there's no guarantee we're going to make it.

The board clearly thinks it's a legitimate offer.

So why did they leave the decision to us?

They want to see if we've got the fire in our bellies.

What?

They want to know if we're really committed to the company and to each other.

Joseph spoke up.

Sounds like a gut check.

Well, I for one vote no!

Same here!

Nick nodded.

So did Kathryn and Joseph.

Jan, what do you say?

Green Banana? Are you kidding?

HA HA HA HA HA HA HA HA HA HA

What impressed Joseph the most, though, were the incredibly passionate debates they got into after that. He'd never seen a team go after each other so hard and come up with crystal-clear agreements and do it without lasting bitterness.

They even called each other on the carpet in ways that startled him, but they always kept the discussion focused on results.

By the session's end, Joseph knew he'd joined one of the most unusual and productive executive teams around—and he couldn't wait to become an active part of it.

the march

Over the next year, DecisionTech's sales grew dramatically. The company met its revenue goals three quarters out of four, and moved into a virtual tie for the industry's top spot.

Performance was up and turnover was down. And except for a temporary dip when they missed their numbers, morale was way up. During that downward tick, the chairman even called Kathryn and told her not to get discouraged.

DecisionTech now had 250 employees. With a new head of sales and HR director on board, Katherine's staff had swelled to eight. It was time to trim the number of her direct reports.

She could handle the weekly one-on-ones, but holding fluid and substantive discussions with eight other people was hard. Problems were bound to surface.

So more than a year after the final Napa off-site, Kathryn revamped DecisionTech's organizational chart.

Nick took back the title of COO—one he finally felt he had earned.

Carlos and Cheryl Gray, the new sales VP, would report to Nick and drop off the CEO's staff.

HR would report to Jan.

That left Kathryn with five direct reports: Martin as CTO, Jan as CFO, Nick as COO, Joseph as VP of marketing, and Jeff as VP of business development.

A week later at the two-day quarterly staff meeting, everyone quickly noticed that Jeff wasn't in attendance.

Hey, where's Jeff?

That's what I wanted to talk to you about.

Jeff won't be coming to these meetings anymore.

Everyone was stunned. What was up?

Jeff quit?

No.

Oh, no—you didn't fire him, did you?!

Kathryn smiled.

For heaven's sake, why would I do that? He'll just be reporting to Nick from now on. Given his new role, we both agreed that made more sense.

The relief on everyone's face was plain, but something was still bothering them.

Jan couldn't hold back.

Kathryn, I'm sure that's true, and no doubt Nick is happy to have Jeff on his team . . .

. . . but won't Jeff be upset that he's not one of your direct reports anymore?

I mean, we're supposed to avoid the ego and status thing, but he's a founder and board member. Did you consider that?

Guys, this was Jeff's idea!

Oh!

Jeff said he loved this team, but being part of Nick's was more logical.

In fact, he insisted it was the right thing to do, both for the team and for the company.

I think we owe it to him—and everyone else at DecisionTech—to make this work. So let's get started!

The Model

Trust is the heart of a cohesive team. Teamwork is impossible without it.

TRUST

Unfortunately, the word *trust* is used and misused so often that it has lost impact and focus.

The ability to predict a person's behavior based on past experience is one aspect of trust.

HI! HI!

PROFILE
JAN ME[
EDUCATION:
EXPERIENCE:

In the context of team-building, trust means the team members know their team mates won't use their vulnerabilities against them. Those vulnerabilities include:

- Skill deficiencies
- Interpersonal weaknesses
- Mistakes
- Requests for help

This concept may sound "soft," but in fact team members only stop guarding themselves when they are truly comfortable.

That frees them to focus all their energy and attention on the job at hand.

Achieving vulnerability-based trust is hard, because people quickly learn to compete with their peers and protect their reputations.

Turning off those instincts, however, is essential.

Teams that lack trust waste time and energy managing their behaviors and interactions.

They dread team meetings, and seldom ask for help or offer to help others.

Morale on distrusting teams is usually low, and unwanted turnover is high.

Members of **teams that don't trust each other** also conceal their weaknesses and mistakes, and seldom offer advice outside their areas of responsibility. They suspect the worst of each other, hold grudges, fail to recognize and tap into each other's skills and experiences, and find reasons to avoid spending time together.

Members of **trusting teams** admit their weaknesses and mistakes, and take risks in offering feedback and assistance. They tap into everyone's experience and skills, devote time and energy to important issues rather than politics, and apologize without hesitation. They also look forward to meetings and other chances to work as a group.

SUGGESTIONS FOR OVERCOMING DYSFUNCTION 1

Vulnerability-based trust isn't created overnight. It takes shared experiences over time, proven follow-through and credibility, and a deep understanding of your team members.

A focused approach, however, can accelerate the process. These tools will help:

Personal histories exercise

This low-risk exercise requires team members to answer questions about their siblings, hometown, unique challenges in childhood, hobbies, first job, and worst job. It helps them relate to each other as human beings with interesting lives, breaks down barriers, and encourages greater empathy.

Minimum time required: 30 minutes

Team effectiveness exercise

Team members speak about the most important contribution each of their peers makes, and one behavior that should be altered or eliminated. This exercise involves more risk, but can extract a great deal of constructive information. Even a relatively dysfunctional team can do it with surprisingly little tension.

Minimum time required: 60 minutes

Personality and Behavioral Preference Profiles

Profiles of behavioral preferences and personality styles are among the most effective tools for building trust, and produce practical and scientifically valid behavioral descriptions of how people think, speak and act. They are non judgmental, based on substantial research, and participants identify their own types. Note: Have a licensed consultant on hand to avoid misusing their powerful implications and applications.

Minimum time required: 4 hours

360-degree feedback

These tools can produce powerful results but are riskier because they call for peers to judge each other openly. I suggest divorcing your 360-degree program from compensation and performance evaluations so it doesn't take on political overtones. Instead, use it to identify strengths and weaknesses.

Experiential team exercises

Rope courses and other experiential team activities offer benefits from doing something rigorous outdoors that involves collective effort and cooperation. These exercises can enhance teamwork if combined with more fundamental and relevant processes.

THE ROLE OF THE LEADER

To encourage trust, a leader must demonstrate vulnerability.

Risking a loss of face in front of the team encourages subordinates to do the same.

But be careful: a leader who fakes vulnerability to manipulate the actions and emotions of others will quickly lose the team's trust.

DYSFUNCTION 2: FEAR OF CONFLICT

All great relationships—including marriages, parenthood, friendships and business—need productive conflict to thrive.

Unfortunately, conflicts at work are often viewed as taboo . . .

. . . and the higher up the management ladder you go, the more people avoid the passionate debates great teams require.

Knowing the difference between productive conflict and destructive infighting is vital.

Productive ideological conflict limits exchanges to plans and ideas. Personal attacks are out, but team members will still argue and get frustrated and emotional.

Outsiders might see this as pure discord, but good teams know that the purpose is to find the best solution in the shortest time.

They discuss and resolve issues quickly and completely and emerge from heated debates with no ill feelings or collateral damage, ready to tackle the next critical issue.

Teams may avoid open ideological conflict so no one's feelings get hurt.

Ironically, they often use back-channel attacks, which are far nastier and harmful than direct confrontation.

Healthy conflict actually saves time and energy.

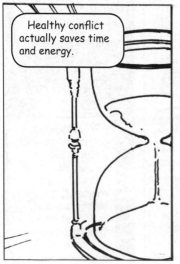

Avoiding conflict in the name of efficiency actually dooms a team to revisiting painful issues with no resolution. Telling someone to take an issue "off-line" is often code for this wasteful syndrome.

As long as team members believe this interplay is bad and unnecessary, healthy conflict is unlikely.

How can a team develop the willingness and ability to engage in healthy conflict?

Below are some simple methods that make conflict more accepted, common and productive.

Teams that fear conflict waste lots of time and energy posturing and managing interpersonal risk. Their meetings are boring because they ignore controversial topics critical to their success, but outside the boardroom back-channel politics and personal attacks thrive. They also fail to tap into the perspectives of all team members.

Teams that engage in conflict have lively, interesting meetings, put critical topics on the table for discussion, and solve real problems quickly. They also minimize internal politics and extract and exploit the ideas of everyone on the team.

SUGGESTIONS FOR OVERCOMING DYSFUNCTION 2

Conflict Mining

Assign the role of "conflict miner" to someone prior to a meeting or discussion. Conflict miners brings buried disagreements to light, so they'll need objectivity, the courage to get the team to work through sensitive issues, and the persistence to keep things moving until the conflict is resolved.

159

Real-time permission

Team members need to coach each other to pursue healthy debate. Whenever people are uncomfortable with the level of discord, it helps to remind each other why conflict is necessary. This drains tension and gives the participants the confidence to continue.

Other tools

The personality style and behavioral preference tools mentioned earlier include descriptions of how different people deal with conflict, and can help you anticipate reactions. A tool specifically for evaluating conflict, the Thomas-Kilmann Conflict Mode Instrument, allows people to approach conflict strategically.

THE ROLE OF THE LEADER

One of a leader's most problematic impulses is the urge to protect team members from harm.

Like overprotective parents who stop their children from arguing, leaders often cut disagreements prematurely short.

Unfortunately, that prevents team members from developing good conflict management skills, strains relationships, and leaves everyone hungry for resolution.

Leaders need to allow the team to sort situations out themselves, even when things get loud and messy.

A leader also has to walk the walk. If you avoid conflict when it is necessary and productive—something all too many executives do—you're allowing this dysfunction to survive and even thrive.

Great teams realize the danger of obsessively seeking consensus, and find ways to achieve buy-in. They know that reasonable people only want their opinions considered and don't need to get their way to support a decision.

People will then rally behind whatever decision the group makes. In an impasse, the team leader makes the call.

CONSENSUS

Great teams also pride themselves on committing to a clear course of action.

They know that making a bold decision and changing direction with equal boldness if they're mistaken is far better than waffling.

CERTAINTY

Dysfunctional teams hedge their bets, delaying until they believe they have enough data to guarantee they're making the right move. While that seems prudent, it actually produces a dangerous paralysis.

Remember, conflict creates a willingness to commit without perfect information. Teams often possess all the data they need, but have to extract it through unfiltered debate.

Only when everyone has put their opinions and perspectives on the table can the team confidently commit to a course of action.

This dysfunction creates dangerous ripple effects when an executive team fails to achieve total buy-in.

Small gaps between top executives become major discrepancies by the time they reach employees below, who try to interpret marching orders that are out of sync with what colleagues in other departments are receiving.

A team that fails to commit loses direction and lacks priorities. Members over-analyze and delay decisions, frequently letting windows of opportunity close. That destroys confidence, inspires a fear of failure, and sets up a culture of second-guessing the moves they make and who makes them.

A team that commits aligns around common objectives and makes its direction and priorities clear. It moves forward without hesitation, takes advantage of opportunities before competitors do, learns from its mistakes, and changes direction without hesitation or guilt.

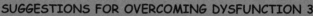

SUGGESTIONS FOR OVERCOMING DYSFUNCTION 3

A team can ensure commitment by maximizing clarity and ensuring buy-in, and resisting the lures of consensus and certainty.

These simple, effective tools and principles will help:

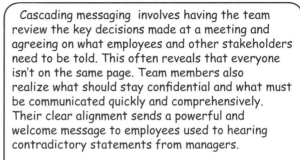

Cascading messaging

Cascading messaging involves having the team review the key decisions made at a meeting and agreeing on what employees and other stakeholders need to be told. This often reveals that everyone isn't on the same page. Team members also realize what should stay confidential and what must be communicated quickly and comprehensively. Their clear alignment sends a powerful and welcome message to employees used to hearing contradictory statements from managers.

Minimum time required: 10 minutes

Deadlines

Ambiguity is the worst enemy of a team that finds it tough to commit. Setting and honoring hard deadlines is essential to ensuring commitment. Interim decisions and milestones are just as vital as final deadlines, since they help identify and address any conflicts before the costs become too great.

Contingency and worst-case scenario analysis

A team with commitment issues should discuss contingency plans up front or, better yet, clarify the worst-case scenario a decision will produce. This usually calms their fears, since they realize a bad decision is survivable and probably less damaging than anticipated.

Commitment-phobic teams can exercise decisiveness on low-risk issues. Teams that make decisions after lengthy discussions but little research or analysis find they make better-than-expected decisions. Research and analysis are important, of course, but teams with this dysfunction tend to overrate their value.

165

How does this fit in with dysfunction #4, avoidance of accountability? Basically, team members must know what the standards are before they can call each other on inappropriate behaviors and actions.

DYSFUNCTION 4: AVOIDANCE OF ACCOUNTABILITY

In the context of teamwork, accountability refers to the willingness of team members to call their peers on actions that might hurt the team.

This dysfunction arises because team members can't handle the difficult conversations and strong emotions typical of confrontations.

Great teams recognize and overcome these natural reactions and willingly enter the danger zone.

166

That's easier said than done, of course, even among very cohesive teams.

In fact, team members who are particularly close may hesitate to hold each other accountable to avoid jeopardizing the relationship.

FRIENDSHIP

Ironically, that only damages ties when someone doesn't live up to expectations.

Great teams bond by holding one another accountable. This demonstrates mutual respect.

Peer pressure is the most effective way to maintain high performance standards.

PEER PRESSURE

Accountability also reduces the company's need to manage employee performance and take corrective action.

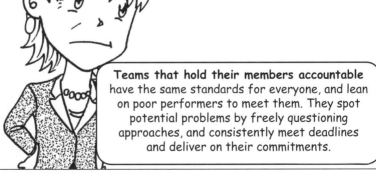

A team that avoids accountability encourages mediocrity, especially when poor performers aren't pressured to improve and the team leader is the sole source of discipline. It also misses deadlines and fails on key deliverables.

Teams that hold their members accountable have the same standards for everyone, and lean on poor performers to meet them. They spot potential problems by freely questioning approaches, and consistently meet deadlines and deliver on their commitments.

167

Publication of goals and standards

Ambiguity is the enemy of accountability. Being clear about what the team needs to achieve, who needs to deliver what, and how everyone should behave makes it easier for team members to hold each other accountable. It is also important to keep those agreements visible so no one forgets.

How can a team ensure accountability? With these management tools, which are as effective as they are simple.

Simple and regular progress reviews

A little structure helps people take action, especially when giving feedback on performance. Team members should communicate constantly about their relative performance against stated objectives and standards. Relying on team members to do that on their own allows them to avoid accountability.

Team rewards

Shifting rewards away from individual performance to team achievement creates a culture of accountability, because team members are unlikely to stand by quietly and fail when a peer is not pulling his or her own weight.

What else would a team focus on? Team status and individual status are the prime candidates.

Plenty of teams—including political groups, famous firms, and even non-profit orgs—succumb to the lure of status.

Their members find success in merely being associated with the organization. Achieving specific results might be desirable but not worthy of self-sacrifice or inconvenience.

TEAM STATUS

People tend to focus on their own interests at the expense of team goals. Successful teams make collective results more important than individual goals.

INDIVIDUAL STATUS

Many teams also focus primarily on survival rather than striving to achieve meaningful objectives. And unfortunately, no amount of trust, conflict, commitment or accountability can overcome that lack of desire to win.

A team that doesn't focus on collective results stagnates, and achievement-oriented employees leave as the company loses its competitive edge. Team members also become easily distracted as they focus on personal goals.

Teams that focus on collective results minimize selfish behavior. They avoid distractions, compete more successfully, and hold on to achievement-oriented staff.

171

A team can ensure a focus on collective results by making those goals clear and only rewarding the behaviors and actions that contribute to them.

Publication of goals and standards

Athletes who publicly state that their team will tear a rival apart cause coaches to gnash their teeth and provoke opponents. Business teams, however, should openly predict progress and success, because they are then more likely to pursue them with unbridled passion.

Results-based rewards

Tying rewards—especially compensation—to specific outcomes helps ensure that team members focus on collective results. Giving a bonus to someone who has achieved no notable results simply because they tried hard tells people that the goal wasn't so important after all.

THE ROLE OF THE LEADER

The leader must focus on collective results. If the team senses that the leader values personal goals more, they'll feel free to do the same.

team leader
- *focused*
- *selfless*
- *objective*

Team leaders must also be selfless and objective, and reserve rewards and recognition for those who truly serve group goals.

- **recognizing contributions and achievement of group goals**

Successful teamwork ultimately comes down to following a set of principles over a long period, and embracing common sense with uncommon levels of discipline, persistence and openness.

By acknowledging their human imperfections, great teams overcome the natural tendencies that make trust, conflict, commitment, accountability, and a focus on results so elusive.

Ironically, great teams succeed because they are exceedingly human.

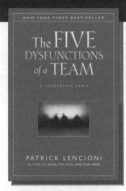
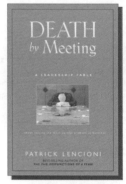
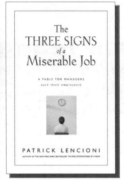
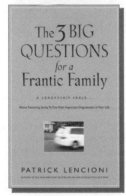
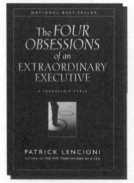
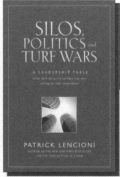